Guide to Watch Flipping

By Amanda Symonds

2nd edition

Copyright © Amanda Symonds 2022

Introduction

So, you want to start flipping watches? Well, you've come to the right place! In this guide, I will teach you everything you need to know about flipping watches for profit. I will cover where to find good deals on watches, how to spot a good deal, and where to sell them for the best price.

What is watch flipping?

Watch flipping is the business of buying and selling watches. It can be a very profitable endeavor, but it requires some knowledge and expertise to do it well. This guide will teach you the basics of watch flipping, including how to find good deals on watches and where to sell them for a profit. With a little practice, you can easily make a part-time or full-time income from watch flipping.

How to start flipping watches

When you flip watches, you are essentially acting as a middleman between buyers and sellers. You find good deals on watches, usually from online sources such as eBay, and then sell them to people who are willing to pay more for the watch than you paid. The key to making money from watch flipping is to find authentic watches that are in high demand and sell them for a profit.

The first step to flipping watches is finding good deals on watches. There are a few ways to do this, but the best way is to find watch dealers who are willing to give you a discount for buying in bulk. You can also find watch companies that sell overstock or discontinued models at deeply discounted prices. Once you have found a few good sources for watches, you need to learn how to spot a good deal. This takes a bit of practice, but with time you will be able to quickly assess whether a watch is underpriced and likely to sell for a profit.

I would probably set a budget, probably between $500-1000 for the first watch and see what you can pick up. It depends on your location and supply and demand for the watch. You have to start somewhere and decide not to be greedy on the first trade. You might pocket $40 or $400 dollars when you flip a watch - however it will realistically be more around $150-200 (especially for your averaged pre-owned or restored watches).

So, buying your first watch for $500 and selling it for $700 would be a success! It might be a good strategy to look for brand names in VGC without a box and look to buy one to flip it. I have seen a business selling vintages boxes on eBay.com. The vintage Rolex boxes with booklets sell consistently between $350-400, Bulova boxes between $70-80, Seiko boxes between $8-50 and Omega boxes between $130-160 (March 2022 figures). Buying original boxes on eBay can increase your sale price by $500-1000 easily.

Luxury watches that cost $5k upwards are a danger to newbies as there are less buyers at this level because they're already priced so tremendously high! Often buyers consider watches in this range and then buy another luxury watch (which is new). Not a good idea to start at the price range.

Ways to add value to your watch

1. you "add value" via repair, cleaning, restoration (e.g., buying broken watches cheap and fixing them). I'd polish them, replace bad crystals, put on new straps, and sell them right back on eBay. You need to be given the right tools and skills or hire someone who has them.

or

2. arbitrage (e.g., buying low in one region and selling high elsewhere).

or

3. random good luck (e.g., finding something cheap at a pawn shop or listed incorrectly on eBay)

This is advice from a Watch Flipper on watchuseek.com, but #2 and #3 seem like false lures. Given how huge and liquid the watch markets are here on watchuseek.com and eBay, I wouldn't imagine many arbitrage opportunities. Good luck is too erratic to pull off consistently, as are talking about a consistent source of income that pays the rent. Unless someone is doing repair work, I suspect a lot of "flipping" is just "churning with a lot of long-run small gains and small losses."

Where to buy and sell watches to flip

There are many places to buy and sell watches, but the most important thing is to find a place where you can get good deals on watches and where there is a demand for the type of watch you are selling. One of the best places to buy watches is online watch forums, such as watchuseek.com. These forums are full of watch enthusiasts who are always discussing watch flipping, deals and scams. They will confirm rules about resale value of near new watches, and give you guidance. Generally, you can ask between 50% and 66% of the RRP for the price of a 12-month-old watch. If the watch has had more than one owner, is still in excellent condition and is older than 12 months, then negotiate a cheaper price than 50% of RRP.

Sites you should check

WatchRecon is 'the most intelligent and comprehensive search engine for private watch sales". It features popular brands like Helios, Omega, Rolex Seiko Zenith Tag Heuer but there's a wide range of other names that you will find here from A-Z (and even some harder to locate). If this sounds interesting then be sure register as new user because only registered members can post items up on their site or app right now!

Chrono24 is the ultimate watch-buying destination for collectors, enthusiasts and professionals alike. Whether you're looking to buy your next reliable timepiece or just want some ideas on what type of vintage pieces are out there Chrono makes it easy! They offer nearly 515k watches from 128 countries with over 100K sold every month - that's an amazing statistic considering they serve as both buyer's market AND seller platform too which means everyone wins in this transaction.

eBay

While it is becoming more difficult to turn a profit by selling watches on eBay, the site still has plenty of rare gems and great deals. Know past prices by search for completed auctions and sales of your preferred watch models. Contact dealers on eBay and ask them to let you know when a vintage watch becomes available and you may get in early.

Watch buyers often set alerts when an item is listed based off what they're searching - so they get notified and start messaging the buyer and asking questions to build rapport and check authenticity before bidding. Look for bad pictures and see if they can message through new pictures showing the condition. You can also ask if the seller can switch on Make Offer and you can make an offer lower than their Buy It Now price. Use these tactics to get a good deal and show a seller you are interested early. This works well when sellers are disgruntled spouses (getting divorced who are selling their exes watch) and don't know about the importance of taking a good photo and don't know the value of the watch.

eBay tip: Watch buyers often set alerts on their phone for when an item becomes available based on their search query. The more models you are looking for, the better change you can pick up a good deal that may be poorly advertised. I also include common misspellings in my eBay watch alerts so I can win the watch that no-one saw!

You can also find deals at watch stores, pawn shops, and online watch dealers. It's important to compare prices between different sellers to make sure you're getting the best deal possible. You can also get discounts on watches by following watch dealers on social media. Many watch dealers offer special discounts to their followers, so it's worth following them to stay up-to-date on the latest deals.

Once you've found a few good sources for watches, you need to decide where to sell them. The best place to sell watches is online, through sites like eBay or Craigslist. You can also sell watches on watch forums, but there are rules and be sure to do your research first to make sure you are selling to a reputable buyer.

I wouldn't attempt to buy and sell the same watch on the same website or forum, especially if it is within a few weeks. People may recognize it and may resent you selling the watch on and making a profit if they missed out the first time it was offered.

When it comes time to sell your watches, there are several places you can go. Online auction sites like eBay are a great option, as are watch stores and pawn shops. Read our detailed explanation below.

You can also sell watches to online watch dealers. Just be sure to research the dealer before selling to them to make sure they are legitimate and will pay you a fair price for your watches. See if there is any feedback online for this dealer. If you can see comments on Facebook ask the dealer about specific watches, as these 'customers or sellers' by direct message

whether they dealt with this watch dealer
and whether they had a good experience.

How to spot a fake (Omega)

You should study what are the characteristic genuine features of the watches you plan to resell. The fastest way to tell is to weigh it!!

We are using an Omega watch below as an example.

If you're in the market for an Omega watch, it's important to know how to spot a fake. There are many knock-off watches on the market, and if you're not careful, you may end up with a watch that's worth much less than you paid for it. In this chapter, we will discuss 10 ways to tell if your Omega is a fake. Stay safe and don't get scammed!

1. Check for Omega's signature on the watch face. All Omega watches have Omega's logo and name engraved on the watch face, so look closely to ensure it is there.

2. Feel for quality craftsmanship. Omega puts a lot of effort into making sure its watches are top-notch — from the materials used to the finishing touches. Fake Omega watches don't go through this process and may feel flimsy or cheaply made in comparison.

3. Inspect any accompanying paperwork closely. Many knock-off Omega watches come with fake documents that look like they came from Omega but are actually just copied images or documents meant to fool buyers into thinking they are getting an authentic product when they're not.

4. Check for Omega's crown logo on the clasp. Omega watches have a distinct crown logo etched into their clasps, so look for it to make sure you're getting an authentic product.

5. Carefully examine all engravings and marks made onto the watch face and body. Omega puts great effort into its designs —

so any imperfections in engraving or markings should be a cause for concern if you think your watch may be fake.

6. Make sure to check the weight of the watch. Omega watches are made with quality materials and can feel heavier than counterfeit ones due to this fact alone.

7. Look at the font used for Omega's name on the watch face. Omega pays close attention to detail, and fonts used for Omega's name should be consistent across all of its watches. If you see that the font is different than usual, this could be a sign that your Omega is fake.

8. Make sure the watch's movement is certified by Omega. Omega uses several types of movements in their watches, and they are all certified by Omega prior to release. So if you suspect your Omega is a fake, make sure to ask for certification information or take it to a professional who can check it out for you.

9. See if there are any visible signs of tampering on the watch case or band. Fake Omega watches are often made with inferior materials and may have visible signs of tampering or wear and tear.

10. Be wary of Omega watches that are priced too low. Omega watches are quite

expensive, so if you find one that is being sold significantly lower than the retail price, it could very well be a fake.

A real scam story from Reddit

" I got scammed on WatchExchange. Here is some advice for first time buyers. I was a long time lurker that finally worked up the courage to pull the trigger on a watch, and I got scammed on r/WatchExchange. I'm not posting this as a sob story but wanted to share some pretty obvious lessons I learned for any first-time watch buyers. Hindsight is always 20/20 and I should have seen the red flags."

"You're not buying a watch, you're buying the seller. You hear this often, and it's true. The seller I was dealing with looked legit (has posted on other watch subs, contributed to the conversation / the community, and had Reddit account history), but didn't have any transaction history. A few days after I sent him the money, he deleted his account.

Ask for references and do what you need to do to feel 100% confident that the seller is going to follow through. If you're not 100% confident, be careful.

Protect yourself - pay the fee and use Paypal G&S instead of F&F. This was my biggest mistake and in hindsight is obviously so dumb. I used F&F instead of G&S. Do your research on what your payment recourse is if something goes wrong, and use G&S if you have any doubt. Don't send strangers money with no buyer protection if you don't fully trust them as a seller.

Scammers don't just take the money and run. I talked to this guy about straps and bracelets -- all the info checked out. **He created the tracking number and proactively sent it to me after I paid him, but never brought the item to USPS.**

Scammers will go to great lengths to make you feel like they are legit throughout the whole transaction. Keep your guard up. I'm lucky that this is a financial mistake I can recover from. I know I'm fortunate for that.

Hopefully, these reminders will help someone else avoid a similar or worse situation. Cheers."

How to sell vintage watches

You can choose from a variety of options when it comes time to sell a watch that's no longer working or one that's simply collecting dust in storage somewhere. Some people prefer an online auction site like eBay because they have access to millions of potential buyers worldwide who might be interested in their item. Others may prefer going through a local dealer who specializes in buying used luxury items such as jewelry and watches because there is less competition from other sellers compared with sites like eBay where anyone can list an item for sale at any given time.

Know the value of your vintage watch

You may have a specific brand or model in mind that you would like to sell. If so, you need to know the value of your watch before making plans on how to go about selling. The price can vary dramatically depending on what type of watch and its condition is being sold. You can't expect to get top dollar unless you have the original box, papers and perhaps even an original receipt of purchase. Not only are people getting better at identifying fakes and scams, but no one wants to buy from a seller who is not thorough in his or her paperwork and knowledge of the product they're selling. So learn about your watch too and be able to tell a good story about why it's a great model.

For example, if your vintage Rolex watch "Rolex Submariner" is from the 1950s and in excellent condition, it would be worth a lot more than a Submariner made just last year. It's important to do your research before selling so you don't end up selling your watch for less than its true value.

Searching in https://www.eBay.com/ watches for Completed Listings featuring your model of watch is a great starting point to see its value and rarity.

Consider what you are willing to sell your vintage watch for.

There are numerous ways to find the right buyer, and it is important to price your watch accordingly. If you are not sure what the watch is worth, there are a few resources that can help you determine a fair asking price.

One of the best ways to sell your vintage watches is through online auction houses and websites like eBay. This allows potential buyers from all over the world to see your watch and make a bid.

Another option is to sell your watch to a dealer or collector. This can be a more personal transaction, but it may also yield a higher price for your watch.

eBay

When most people think of online auction sites to sell antique watches, eBay is usually the first site that comes to mind. This makes sense because it's one of the largest sites on the internet for buying and selling all types of items including watches. Some so many potential buyers who visit this site every day looking for vintage watches just like yours!

If you want to sell your watch quickly, then eBay is a good option. If you want to get a decent price for your watch, then it will be a little more difficult. Before listing, search on eBay.com/watches to see if there is to be competition from other sellers who have similar watches listed at a cheaper price than you are looking for, in case this can limit your final sale value.

If so don't see any competition, then you are good to go!

Local Dealer

If you're looking for a more personalized selling experience, then going through a local dealer might be the best option for you. There are many independent watch dealers who specialize in buying and selling used luxury watches. They will usually have a website or storefront where you can browse their current inventory.

One of the benefits of dealing with a local dealer is that they are more likely to offer a better price for your watch than what you would get from an online auction site like eBay. This is because there is less competition from other sellers and they don't have to worry about paying for shipping or being scammed by a dishonest buyer.

Retail Stores

Another option is selling your antique watch through a retail store. These are usually smaller shops that aren't dedicated to buying secondhand watches but they will buy from customers if the price is right.

This option is great for people who want to get rid of their watch quickly because you won't have to wait until your item sells on eBay or with a local dealer. You can go into the store, Make Offer, and have cash in your hands to spend on whatever you want.

Sell your vintage watches the right way!

Now that you know a few different ways to sell your vintage Rolex watches, it's time to choose the best option for you. Do some research on what similar watches are selling for and price your watch accordingly. If you're not sure about the value of your watch, there are plenty of resources available online to help you out.

From the list above you can see that there is no single right or wrong way to go about selling vintage watches, but it's important to do some research before listing them online so you don't end up getting less than what they're worth!

Alternatively, if getting top dollar for your vintage timepiece is more important than how fast it sells, then selling antique watches through an online auction house or websites like eBay and a local dealer would be your best choice.

Sell your Vintage Watches the right way with these tips and tricks

· Know the worth of your watch. Do some research before you sell it so that you have a good idea of what to ask for.

· Clean your watch before selling it. This will make it look nicer and may increase its value.

· Include items that increase the value, such as the manual, an original box and a service certificate from a licensed watch dealer. Some watch shops will provide a valuation certificate for a nominal fee and this can help get you a fair price for your watch. Having an original receipt of purchase can also help.

· Look to buy original boxes on eBay as this can increase your sale price by $500-1000 easily.

· List the reasons why people would want to buy it. Think about what makes your watch so special and list its benefits on the sales page. You may also include some photos of this watch in action if you have them available.

· Learn about your watch too and be able to tell a good story about why it's a great model. Put this information in the listing so it looks as good as possible.

· Be sure to list all details about the vintage watches you are selling, including any flaws or defects that they may have. This will give potential buyers more information about what they can expect to receive when buying from you. If necessary, offer returns for items purchased on eBay so that buyers can trust your listings.

· Take good photos of the watch you are selling and include them in your listing. This will help attract more customers to your page and increase sales! Be sure that the lighting is good for taking pictures, as this can also affect how appealing it appears to potential customers. Try taking a few different shots of your watch so that you can get the best possible pictures.

· Include keywords that people are searching for in your subject and description. This will trigger alert notifications for watch collectors and buyers.

· Think about a promoted listing on eBay if you see that other people are using this tactic to get sales.

Selling a vintage watch can be a great way to make some extra money, but it's important to do your research first and choose the right selling method. By following these tips, you can ensure that you get the best price for your watch while also providing potential buyers with all the information they need to make a decision.

What are the expenses involved in a watch flipping business?

Overall, watch flipping is a fairly low-cost business to get into. There are some initial expenses, but once you have established a few good sources for watches, the only other costs involved are the occasional repair or service job.

If you sell watches to another dealer then you should expect to give them a cut under the market value. The dealer will then sell it at a higher price and make their money on the margin.

If you buy vintage watches for resale then they need to be serviced and repaired then you may need to factor in these costs. You should be prepared to buy your own tools to open the watch and do basic checks and be able to wind automatic watches.

Other expenses involved in watch flipping vary depending on how you choose to do business. If you buy and sell watches online, you will need to pay for shipping and handling. If you sell watches at a physical location, you will need to pay for rent, utilities, and other related expenses.

You should also factor in the cost of insuring your watch collection. This is especially important if you are storing watches at a physical location.

Is it possible to restore any watch?

Almost always, yes. Any timepiece may be serviced, whether it is glass or crystal, vintage or contemporary, automatic or manual. It becomes more difficult to repair a watch as it gets older; however, it can usually be done so long as you find the appropriate repair shop or can salvage parts from another watch of the same model.

What is the cost of servicing a vintage timepiece??

A full overhaul should come with a guarantee of one to two years to ensure that the timepiece functions properly throughout normal use. The cost of an overhaul varies depending on the manufacturer, but it generally starts at $250 and may reach $1,000 or more for a vintage timepiece.

Watch repair tools that flippers need

Here is a list of the most useful items you should have:

1. Watch Case Opener
2. Watchmakers Screwdriver Set
3. Watchmakers Tweezers
4. Eyeglass or Eye Loupe
5. Watch Hand Lifting Levers
6. Movement Holder
7. Parts Container
8. Pegwood
9. Glass Benzine Jar and Watch Degreasing Fluid
10. Rubber Dust Blower

11. Watch Oils and Greases, Oilers and Oil Pots

12. Rodico Cleaning Putty

Horotec and Bergeon make excellent movement holders, screwdriver sets and tweezers.

Pegwood is used for a number of tasks within the watch repair trade but the two main uses are for cleaning out jewel holes and watch parts before cleaning the watch with chemicals, and for holding down parts and springs during assembly and reassembly.

Rodico is a cleaning putty that has thousands of uses but it's mostly used for removing fingerprints, oil, dirt and grime from your watch movement.

Rodico works just like a pencil eraser simply wipe or dab it onto your watch movement to discover its benefits. Another great use for this wonderful putty is for lifting out hard to grab jewels or screws from your movement.

Let's talk about some of these in detail:

Clean cloth

Watch enthusiasts know the importance of keeping their timepieces pristine. To clean these delicate items, you should use a dry cloth and never press hard on any part that may damage its surface scratched by an object such as pen/pencil leads while writing with them.

Ultrasonic cleaners

Other cleaning equipment can include ultrasonic cleaners.

A diligent watchmaker disassembles every part of the watch he is servicing by removing the tiny screws which hold the watch together and puts every element in an ultrasonic machine to clean them - or use other liquids if there are traces of rust to remove.

A watchmaker's ultrasonic cleaning machine is somewhat similar to the ones used for cleaning jewelry, glasses and such at home. The tiny pieces are put into metal holding containers, and then ultrasonically cleaned until they become shiny as new. The watchmaker then carefully checks every jewel, so to see if the watch is performing well. If he finds something odd, like an ovalized hole in a jewel, meaning that there is an issue in the watch, which could be serious and require some more costly repair (like substituting the jewel or finding a spare part to replace the faulty one).

If everything is ok, he reassembles back the watch, piece by piece, adding special mineral oil when needed to lubricate the mechanism.

Loupe

When you invest in a luxury watch to resell with a high-end movement, it is essential to have the right tools for your inspection. A loupe and magnifying glass are both good options so that intricate details can be inspected easily without having any problem seeing what's on display or working behind the scenes respectively.

Case wrench

A case wrench, like a screwdriver, will press fit small pins into the back of the watch and twist it back. Using a watch case holder to keep the timepiece safely while you turn the tool might help. The crystal or case press, for example, will press on friction watch backs and install watches crystals in the same manner as another watch.

Electronic Winders

The best automatic watch winders will automatically keep your watch running by gently revolving it at regular intervals. With an exotic manual option for those who prefer to do things the old-fashioned way, these devices ensure that you never have a dead battery when on the go.

Watch Safe

Too many people have stories about timepieces being stolen. To prevent this it is typically a good idea to invest in a safe. Watch lovers are lucky because a whole universe of "horological safes" exist that come complete with special drawers and even winders. Watch safes are a more expensive item but can easily justify themselves if they prevent just one robbery attempt.

Rate Result Machine

These high-quality machines often called timing clocks or beat rate testers for timepieces are used to make sure that a watch's accuracy is at its highest possible level. They will tell you if your timepiece needs repairs and also serve as an indicator of how fast or slow it runs in beats per minute (BPM).

Can you really make part-time income flipping watches?

With a little practice, watch flipping can be a very profitable business. It's a great way to make some extra money or even a part-time income. Just be sure to do your research and always get the best deals possible on watches.

Build your contacts in the profession to help you if you buy a watch that doesn't work and you need some parts, or a valuation over the phone from a reputable dealer (before you buy). They can help you avoid making mistakes that will hurt you in the first 12 months while you are learning the ropes.

How much money you can make from watch flipping also depends on how much time and effort you put into it. With practice, you can easily make a few hundred dollars per month flipping watches. If you are more dedicated, you can make a full-time income from watch flipping.

You would probably need to flip ten watches a month, to make $2K and so you need to have a system in place to find good deals, do repairs and add value and then on-sell them at a profit. So now you understand, watch flipping isn't just something you succeed at without putting a considerate amount of time into learning the craft.

Note, it can be hard to find a new watch model at a discount and then buy several of them to sell at a profit on eBay. You need to test your idea before you buy many pieces (inventory). Others can catch on and then try to undercut you on the same platform, reducing your margin.

Buying and fixing up vintage washes for resale is more sustainable for ongoing income but requires more work to learn the different models.

If you are keen to learn from an ex-watch flipper, check out the below video for some great tips on how to flip luxury watches.

https://www.youtube.com/watch?v=3Gta9XTeHV8&feature=youtu.be

So, now you know a bit more about watch flipping – what it is, where to find deals on watches, and what the expenses involved are.

Custom Mod Watch Services Guide

Providing a custom mod watch service can be a great addition to your business, and there are many different ways to customize one. In this guide, we'll show you how to understand what watch modding is and whether it is a good side-hustle for you.

Custom watches are becoming increasingly popular these days because they allow people from all walks of life to express their style through their choice of wrist wear. Whether it's vintage-inspired or modernly sleek; there's something out there that everyone can appreciate and enjoy wearing every day. Clients are looking for a stylish timepiece that's perfectly suited for their fashion sense and needs!

What is a custom watch mod?

A custom mod watch is a timepiece that has been customized to meet the buyer's specifications. The term "mod" stems from the world of skateboarding, where it's used to describe the modifications made to a skateboard. The same concept applies when designing a custom watch mod; you'll need be able to produce the specific features and design elements that the custom wants, resulting in a one-of-a-kind timepiece. Of course, you can take orders and outsource this service to one of your contacts who is an experienced watch service and repairer.

Custom mod watches can be made out of sports or luxury brands and may feature unique styles that are not covered by most watch manufacturers.

There is a wide range of aftermarket parts and accessories that are available to help you get the watch's aesthetics you desire, so it's important to do your research and understand what you can buy (and then offer to the customer)

Is watch modding illegal?

In its simplest form, watch modding can involve changing or replacing factory-made parts such as dials, hands, bezels, crowns, cases and straps with different components. It can also include adding features such as luminous material or water resistance enhancements.

Let's look at whether or not it is actually illegal. The answer to this question will depend on where you live and the laws in your jurisdiction. In some countries, modifying any kind of watch may be illegal due to copyright or trademark laws. You need to do your own research on forums.

Additionally, in some countries, it may be illegal to modify a watch without the permission of the original manufacturer or distributor, as this could potentially affect their sales or reputation.

In other countries, however, modding is perfectly legal and can even be done with permission from the original manufacturer.

Generally speaking, if you are legally allowed to buy and own a watch then you should also be legally allowed to modify it for your own personal use. However, it is important to note that modifying a watch may void any existing warranties or guarantees provided by the manufacturer.

With these guidelines in mind, customising and modding watches can be an enjoyable and rewarding hobby for many people.

Some different types of custom watches include:

Luxury brand watches (Rolex, Omega, and Seiko Watch) with unique or customized styles.

Sports brand watches (Nike, Adidas, etc.) with modified or personalized features.

Vintage Mod Watch with modern updates and styling.

Custom Made or Commissioned Mod Watch that is specific to your needs.

Designer Mod Watch with unique materials and features.

5 Popular Custom Mod Watch Brands

Rolex Submariner Watch

It is done with a PVD black or Gun Metal grey finish and a custom laser-engraved bezel. The case is made of 316L stainless steel and has a screw-down crown for water resistance up to 330 feet (100 meters).

Seiko 5 Sports

This watch has a custom wood or bamboo case and leather band. The dial is black with white hands and hour markers. It has a date window at the three o'clock position, luminous dots next to the hour markers, and a mineral crystal. Seiko mod parts are all over the market and can be used to change the look of these high-end watches.

Omega Speedmaster Moonwatch

This is a 42-mm chronograph with stainless steel case and bracelet. The Moonwatch has a Hesalite crystal and is water-resistant to 50 meters. It includes an Omega Calibre 1861 hand-winding mechanical movement, an exhibition case-back and a sapphire crystal.

Casio G-Shock Rangeman watches with custom camouflage band.

This digital watch is shock resistant and has a stopwatch, countdown timer, world time (31 times), sunrise/sunset alerts. The watch also features a GPS navigation system and maps for tracking your current location.

Seiko SKX 007

It is a watch with a custom PVD or DLC black finish, a unique dial, and unique watch hands. It is one of the best affordable Seiko dive watches. It has the classic and desirable diver watch look and is an excellent diving watch that can also be worn on any occasion.

Seiko dive watches are a popular choice for those looking for a high-end watch with subtle modification.

What are the key factors for your client to consider when buying a custom mod watch?

There are several key factors to consider when purchasing a custom mod watch. They include:

Their budget – How much can they afford to spend on a custom mod watch?

The style of the watch – What type of watch do they prefer, and what style will best suit their needs?

The materials used in the construction of the watch – Are they durable and high quality?

Additional features or functions – Do you need a chronograph or tachymeter?

The quality of the workmanship – Is the watch well-made and will it last?

Warranty and aftersales service – What is the warranty policy and what kind of aftersales service is provided? *You need to consider what you will offer here!*

Finally, always remember that quality should be your top priority when producing a custom mod watch. Watch enthusiasts often spend years painstakingly researching their dream watch, so they don't skimp on quality when choosing a custom mod watch of their own.

How do clients find a reputable custom mod watchmaker or retailer?

When looking for a reputable custom mod watchmaker or retailer, clients do their research and ask around for recommendations. They check online reviews to get an idea of the quality of their products and services.

Custom watch mods are often done by skilled craftsmen who have extensive training and experience with watches, to achieve a mod will be of the highest quality. Customize My Watch is an excellent place to get all kinds of customizations for Rolex, G-shocks, Seiko watches etc.

Check their website and see if you can offer alternatives or have a competitive advantage. Can you produce your own website to promote your services?

What is involved in doing a watch mod and what tools do you need?

There are many steps to customizing a timepiece.

Firstly, the parts of your watch that will be modified must be disassembled so they can be worked on more easily. This often requires special tools such as case back openers and pin-pointers.

The next step is to paint, polish, or engrave the new mod parts. This can be done with a variety of tools such as brushes, dremels, and sandpaper.

Finally, the pieces must be reassembled and the watch must be tested to make sure it is still water-resistant and working properly.

Tools required for a watch mod include case back openers, pin-pointers, and jeweler's screwdrivers.

What tools and supplies do I need to do a watch mod?

There are several tools and supplies you'll need when customizing your own watch. They include:

· Case back openers – These are used to remove the backs of the watch's case so you can work on them more easily.

· Jeweler's screwdrivers – These are used to open and close watch screws.

· Pin-pointers – These are small metal detectors that help you find tiny watch parts that have fallen inside the case.

· Brushes – These are used to apply paint, polish, or engraving to watch parts.

- Dremels – These are small rotary tools that can be used to engrave and cut through metal.
- Sandpaper – This is used to smooth down rough surfaces on watch parts.
- Parts cleaner – This is used to clean the inside of cases and get rid of any particles that may cause damage.
- Flathead screwdriver – This is used to remove screws from watch cases.
- Phillips head screwdriver – This is also used to remove screws, but it has a cross-shaped head
- Tweezers – These are used to hold small watch parts while you work on them.

Overall, custom watch mods can be a great way to make a luxury timepiece even more special and unique.

Sometimes you are not able to get replacement parts and so a mod solves the repair problem.

Many benefits of Watch Modding

For watch collectors, modding allows you to express your unique personality and style.

Whether you're into vintage watches or prefer something more modern, you'll be able to find the perfect piece that will help set your look apart from everyone else's. Another advantage of custom mods is that they often come with a lower price tag than luxury watches.

This is because you're not paying for the brand name, but rather the features and design of the watch itself. So, if you're on a budget but still want a high-quality timepiece, then a custom mod watch may be the perfect option for you.

You can improve the appearance of a watch by changing the color or type of your watch strap, adding new bezel inserts, or installing a new dial. You can improve the function of your watch by replacing worn parts such as the sapphire crystal into new crystal and crowns, and adding features like chronographs or tachymeters.

Finally, watch modding is also a great way to commemorate special occasions. If you've just gotten married, had a baby, or reached a major milestone in your life, then consider commissioning a custom mod watch as a unique way to celebrate. You'll be able to choose all the details yourself, making it a truly unique and memorable gift.

Custom watches are often considered investments because they retain value for many years after their original purchase date.

Tips for ensuring that your custom mod is done correctly and safely

When it comes to custom watch mods, there are a few things you can do to ensure that the job is done correctly and safely.

First, always use high-quality materials. This will help to ensure that the watch is durable and looks good for years to come.

Second, make sure the watchmaker is experienced and qualified. This will help to ensure that they have the skills needed for a good job.

Finally, always ask questions and get a detailed list of costs before you begin and accept the modding order. This will help to ensure that the watch is done correctly while staying within everyone's budget and you can make profit on the deal!

Custom watch mods can take time to complete, so don't rush the process. By following these tips, you can guarantee that the custom watch mod will be done correctly and the client will be happy.

FAQ's

Q: What type of watches can be modded?
A: Almost any watch can be modded, from luxury timepieces to sporty G-shocks.

Q: How long does it usually take to complete a watch mod?
A: It depends on the complexity of the mod, but most mods take at least a few days to complete.

Q: What type of tools are required for a watch mod?
A: The tools required for a watch mod include case back openers, jeweler's screwdrivers, pin-pointers, and brushes.

3D printing parts for watches

It is possible to use a 3d printer for making watch repair tools and movement holders. People online have printed holders for several movements, case back knives, watch parts trays and different types tool storage solutions. The most useful has to be a watch back wrench for a Seiko divers.

I printed it with six square pins that fitted the back perfectly, took the very tight back off with ease. I now don't use the metal 3 point wrench.

The case knives printed in PLA work very well, if only lasting for a few uses but with no risk of scratching the watch back. Search on Thingiverse and other libraries for GCODE files.

In a few years, it will be easy and cheap to replicate watch parts that are hard to find or very expensive. You can either make them using 3D software on the computer or use a 3D laser to scan a part that is already available and then make some copies of it.

The plastic parts such as those used on quartz watches are probably easy to make and similar in "strength" to the original ones but I wonder how good the metal parts are compared to the real ones.

Commercial 3D printers can use laser sintering to fuse metal together to make the parts and can make them from cast iron powder, silver, gold, bronze, brass, platinum, titanium, ceramic etc. and can make very strong long, lasting parts.

Shapeways lets you upload your 3D models to it, pick what you want it to be made from and it will give you the price, you pay and a couple of weeks later it turns up in the post. I've never used Shapeways to make commercial parts but the metal samples I ordered felt really strong.

Conclusion

Custom watches are a great way for clients to express their style and individuality. They are in demand for special gifts and a great way to make money in between flips.

Printed in the USA
CPSIA information can be obtained
at www.ICGtesting.com
LVHW011829310723
753929LV00003B/164